AN AUTISM UNSCRIPTED LIFE

TONY HERNANDEZ PUMAREJO

ISBN-13: 978-1723848308
ISBN-10: 1723848301

Contents

DEDICATION

This book is dedicated to all the human beings with Autism and other disabilities that are going through significant life challenges, which a lot of them have been ignored and left behind in society. A disability should never be used against the individual. The goal of the book is to eliminate the erroneous assumption that people with Autism are a liability to society. People with Autism and other disabilities are here to contribute and make a positive and long-lasting difference in the World today. They have the same right to achieve a great life as the rest of society. Let's give these great human beings the opportunity to fulfill their purpose in life.

Also, this book is dedicated to all the pets and animals that have the pleasure of meeting and have a friendship with from childhood to adulthood. Animals have the same rights to live a great life as humans too. Especially, I want to dedicate this book to Cheese, the best dog in the World.

iv

ACKNOWLEDGMENTS

I want to thank my mother, Evelyn Pumarejo, for her unconditional love and support through the good and tough moments in my life. Without her, I wouldn't be here right now to tell my story. Also, I want to thank my father, Julio Hernandez, for his love and support during my life. I also want to thank and recognize my aunt, Neida Pumarejo, for her support, especially as it relates to my career. Also, I want to recognize my older siblings Rachel, Julian and my younger sibling Paul as well as my aunt Wanda Pumarejo for their contributions.

I would like to give a shout out to Donna Lorman, the president of Autism Society of Greater Orlando for giving me the first opportunity to volunteer and make significant contributions to the Autism community. Also, like to give a shout out to Paula Breeden, the president of ASD Adult Achievement Center for giving me the opportunity to help young adults with Autism.

Last, but not least, I would like to give shout outs to the following people who played integral and critical roles in my career and life: Iris Negron, Iniabel Sanchez, Nelly Perez, Vicente Quiñones, Maritza Gaviria, Rosa Alvarez, Terri Walsh, Thomas Walker, Richard Calloway, Pedro Cardona, Tony Marin, Maria McCormick, Lisette Guillen-Dolby, Debbie Wheeler, Gina Bellanco, Penny O'Connell and Stephani Leon.

INTRODUCTION

My full name is Antonio Gabriel Hernandez Pumarejo. But, I simply go by Tony. I was born in Bayamon, Puerto Rico at the Hospital San Pablo on March 3, 1990, according to my birth certificate. I don't limit my life to my biological age. I don't remember much about my early years as a child, but I do remember moments in which I was not behaving like most normal kids. I felt that there was something different about me, but I didn't know exactly what it was nor was very conscious of it.

THE FIRST TEN YEARS (1990-2000)

CHAPTER 1: THE BEGINNING

First thing that I began to identify was that I had verbal impairment. Until the age of 4, I was completely nonverbal. However, there was more to my situation than just verbal impairment. I didn't know exactly what it was, but I had a feeling that I was not like the other kids. I had problems understanding what they did, how they talked, and how they behaved. This led to a great misunderstanding, which eventually led towards me going through severe bullying attacks. I didn't know how to respond correctly due to the difficulty of understanding other people. Because of this, I made a lot of mistakes in responding to different types of situations. I didn't know exactly what was wrong or what condition I had, but I do remember that I had unusual problems.

I got a little bit more of information about the challenges that I had when they enrolled me in the special education program, but still didn't know exactly what I had. During this period, I started going to different types of therapies. From what I remember, I had the following therapies: speech therapy, occupational therapy, and behavior therapy. I went to these therapies until I got into the second grade, which was the year that I was taken out of the special education program completely. Because of the challenges that I had, I was held back for one year of school, meaning that I started kindergarten at the age of 6.

Despite these difficult challenges, there were also good moments during my childhood. At school, I went on different field trips and even had a birthday celebration in my classroom. I remember to my surprise when they celebrated my 5th birthday. The classroom was decorated with a Super Mario theme. As a birthday gift, I received the Super Mario All-Stars video game for Super Nintendo. That day was full of fun and happiness. It is weird for me to remember some experiences of my life clearly and other experiences, I don't remember well, but it is still a mystery for me to this day.

WITH MOM, JULIAN AND RACHEL AT EASTER PARTY

The years that I was in special education were the best years that I had in school life, in contrast to what followed for the rest of my school life. I only had two people that I considered the closest thing to a friend during this period. There was one friend who was a girl, and she went by the name of Ximena. She was my next-door neighbor. I consider her my first "friend" that I had in my life. We had good times, and we played together. I went to her house many times, and her parents were very good with me in the beginning. However, she changed her behavior, and her parents didn't allow me to see her again for unknown reasons. Her mother didn't want her daughter to be associated with a person that was weird and not like the other kids. I reacted angrily to the rejection, but it was not the right thing to do despite the rejection. I never saw her and her family again once they moved out of the neighborhood. After this, I meet another girl at the same school. Her name was Luz. She was funny and a good person. She eventually became my very first best friend. In fact, we were such good friends that our families were also friends as well. My mom and her mom were very close. We had great times like dancing at the kindergarten graduation. She and her family also took care of us after coming back from school in the afternoons while mom was working full time. Then, a sad event happened in my friend's life. Her mother passed away. Not only was it tragic for her and her family, but it was also tragic for me and my family. Her mother was like a mother to me also.

Initially, the first years at Fairview Elementary School (Trujillo Alto, Puerto Rico) were very good. But then after the first grade, my experience got worse. During my last years at this elementary school, I was constantly bullied, and it increased as each day passed by. Even worse, during this time, my mom began to have health problems and had no choice but to leave Puerto Rico. We had to go live with our father in 2000. Back then, I was confused and didn't know what was going on. She was gone for medical treatments for a couple of months and then she moved permanently to Florida in 2001. It was also during this time between 1998 and 2000 that my visits to therapy stopped completely. I never understood the reason why I stopped going to therapies, even though I didn't know exactly what disability I had (my mindset was that I had issues with the way I speak and talk with other people). What I knew then was that I was going to start the fourth grade at a new school. In the beginning, I saw that as something good, because I didn't want to be in my first elementary school anymore, but at the same time, I felt sad because I also had a few good memories there. I was depressed because things were not going to be the same, and I was struggling with the change. It could have been related to the unknown disability that I had, but I didn't know it at the time.

WITH MY MATERNAL GRANDFATHER

WITH MY PATERNAL GRANDFATHER

CHAPTER 2: CHILDHOOD HOBBIES

During my childhood, I was able to cultivate different hobbies. As a kid, I loved to watch Cartoon Network. My initial favorite cartoon shows were The Jetsons and The Flintstones. Then later, my favorite cartoon shows were Cow and Chicken, Johnny Bravo and Dexter's Laboratory and Japanese amines like Dragon Ball Z and Gundam Wing. When I got a little older, I watched fewer cartoons. Another hobby I developed was watching professional wrestling, because my older brother recommended it. He played a game called WWF War Zone for Nintendo 64. We played this game a lot. I also find out that there was a real wrestling show named WWF War Zone, later finding out it was Raw is War. The three wrestlers that I used to play in this game the most were Stone Cold Steve Austin, The Undertaker, and Bret the Hitman Hart. It was in late 1998 that I first started watching wrestling. Later, my mother got me the wrestling video game called "WCW/nWo Revenge." It was here that I find out that there were two wrestling companies: World Wrestling Federation (previously WWF, now WWE) and World Championship Wrestling (WCW). I started watching both wrestling promotions on a weekly basis. My favorite WWF wrestlers were Stone Cold Steve Austin and The Rock. My favorite WCW wrestlers were Goldberg, Bret Hart, and Hulk Hogan. Later, my favorite wrestlers in WWE were Kurt Angle, Shawn Michaels, and Randy Orton. Even though I don't follow wrestling anymore, I never forget the good moments I had with this hobby, and from time to time I play the Fire Pro Wrestling games on PlayStation 3 and PC.

One key hobby that I learned when I was a kid was to play video games. I grew up playing Super Nintendo and Sega Genesis a bit, but mostly I spent time playing the Super Nintendo system. I loved the Super Mario series and I played it together with mom and older siblings all the time. I will never forget those moments of joy. My favorite games were Super Mario World, Super Mario All-Stars, Mario Kart, and Super Star Wars games. Then I got the Nintendo 64, and I played games like Super Mario 64, Diddy Kong Racing, Star Wars (games like Shadows of Empire and Rogue Squadron), WWF WrestleMania 2000, WCW Mayhem, WWF No Mercy and many more.

A hobby that I was not successful in creating was sports. The reason why I never played sports with other people is due to their attitude while playing. Due to difficulty with my disability and not being able to understand people effectively, I was most of the time attacked and bullied while playing sports. That is why I focused on doing other activities like running and riding my bicycle when I was alone.

Another thing that happened during my first ten years was music. I never had a clear or favorite music genre I like. All I did was just focus on the rhythm of the music and listen to what other people listened to in my household. I listened to different songs, even though I was never good at learning the lyrics or the name of the artists singing the songs.

One interesting hobby that I had was to be obsessed with mountains, roads, and bridges. Every time I went to the mountains of Puerto Rico (especially Aibonito, where most of my family was located), I was amazed by the view of the mountains and was focused on the details of the mountains. I also loved going to the Yunque National Forest. I was so obsessed with mountains, roads, and bridges that I also made drawings of them on paper (which resulted in another hobby for me, which was arts). I then proceeded to do drawings, pictures of other things that I liked, for example, Star Wars, video games, wrestling, etc. During 1998-1999, I was enrolled in the "Liga de Arte School" in San Juan, where I took drawing and painting classes. Then years later, I was signed up to take classes at the "Escuela de Artes Plasticas." I have always maintained a fascination with the arts.

Another weird but interesting hobby that I had was being obsessed with the weather. Living on a tropical island, I went through different storms and hurricanes. My obsession with hurricanes led me to think that I wanted to be a meteorologist. I liked tracking the hurricane trajectories and was obsessed with knowing where the hurricane was going. I even made drawings of hurricanes too.

Another thing that I was obsessed with was food. I love the Hispanic food, especially Puerto Rican food, like rice with beans, amarillos, tostones, pork, chicken, ribs, and desserts like flan. At the same time, I was obsessed with junk food, especially getting chicken tenders from Burger King.

AN AUTISM UNSCRIPTED LIFE

When I was a kid, one of the things that I liked family related were the holiday activities. My favorite family activities were Thanksgiving Day, New Year's Day, and Three Kings Day. The best part of these activities was the great food and receiving gifts on Three King's Day. In terms of the food, I loved rice, beans, pork, chicken, tostones, potato salad, amarillos, etc. Not to mention the awesome holiday desserts made at these activities like tembleque and flan. Another thing I enjoyed in childhood was when I went to my maternal grandparents' home. I stayed with them on most weekends. My maternal grandmother cooked French toast for breakfast and cooked great food alongside my maternal aunt, Wanda. One funny thing from my childhood is that I used to love watching *Barney the dinosaur*. One interesting thing about that is that I always got angry when they turned off the TV while Barney was still on or the show ended. This was one pattern – being interrupted – that was part of the condition that I had which I was not conscious of it when I was a kid. These hobbies were great, but there was one important hobby that defined my life forever: Star Wars!

CHAPTER 3: STAR WARS

When I was five years old, I saw the original *Star Wars*; the one released exactly in 1977 on VHS. I didn't know exactly what it was, but they told me that it was a trilogy of movies that talk about the story of Luke Skywalker. The story was that he was trying to become a warrior called a Jedi, with his main purpose to defeat the dark lord called Darth Vader and his evil Empire. Then I proceeded to watch the entire trilogy when I was six years old. I was super impressed, even though I didn't know everything about Star Wars yet. I remember that in 1997, they were going to re-release the Star Wars Trilogy Special Edition in the movie theaters. Unfortunately, I didn't saw them in the movie theater. But the good news was when I got excellent grades in school, my mother gave me as a gift the Star Wars Trilogy Special Edition on VHS. It was one of the best days of my life, and I watched those movies over and over again.

Shortly after that, I went to the Castillo Serrallés in Ponce, Puerto Rico. During my visit, I went to one of the rooms, which the tour guide said that it had a Star Wars Collection. He said during the visit that this was going to be the last time the collection was going to be at the castle. It was a room that belonged to one of the members of the Serralles Family. Once I entered the room, I was astonished in terms of what I saw! Immediately upon entering the room, smoke began to appear like I was entering a spaceship. It was a hallway that would lead to the main room of the collection. Then I entered the main room, where the Star Wars Collection was located. The room was a replica of Echo Base from Hoth (seen at the Empire Strikes Back). I was so impressed by the collection that I committed myself that day to create my own Star Wars Collection, which is still one of my main life goals to this very day. It was that day that I officially became a Star Wars Fan for life. I watched the original trilogy over and over again. It became an important hobby. I was excited when I learned that George Lucas was going to do the prequel trilogy, which would tell the story of Anakin Skywalker, who would later become Darth Vader. *Episode 1: The Phantom Menace* was the first Star Wars movie that I watched in the movie theater. Something that I regretted was that mom purchased Star Wars toys for me, and I didn't take care of them like I should have back then. Then when *Episode 2: Attack of the Clones* was released, it was here that I began to collect Star Wars toys. I tried to create my Star Wars Collection, but I had a difficult time working on the collection due to circumstances. My connection to the Star Wars universe would continue to grow from there and to this day, I am proud to be a Star Wars fan for life.

CHAPTER 4: CHILDHOOD CHALLENGES

One of the more important things to talk about during the first 10 years were my daily struggles. I was a person with a lot of feelings and struggles with interactions with people. I knew that I had issues, and I wasn't like the other kids, but I wasn't sure what kind of disability I had at this point. When I was in my first school, I was most, if not, all the time by myself, suffering from chronic loneliness. Everyone either ignored me or attacked me by bullying me emotionally, mentally, and physically. There were other moments like when we went on a field trip to see a play in a theatre. During the play, an adult from the back pointed at me and told me to shut up and sit down. This person had made me feel so bad that throughout the play I just closed my eyes and didn't watch the rest of the play. Something similar happened when I went with my family to the Discovery Zone, a place where they had an inside playground and arcade machines. I was playing in one of the playgrounds, and when I began to enter a section of the playground, I was told that I should not pass by one of the workers at the place. The problem was that the way she did it made me feel bad and I went out of the playground. I don't know why I took these actions in response to these situations, but once I found out more about what I had, then it made sense. Also, I went through challenging times in my family. My family went through a divorce at the age 5. My relationship with older siblings was not that close during childhood. I had some connection with extended family members on both my mom's and dad's side, but those connections decreased years later. It was very tough for a person with a disability to go through these issues.

TRANSITION ERA (2000-2003)

CHAPTER 5: NEW SCHOOL

I moved in with my father in 2000, which meant that I was going to start a new school. I started the new school with new expectations and the hope that the change of scenery was going to help me solve my problems. Immediately, I saw that I was wrong. I was attacked and bullied immediately at the new school. However, I got along with the teachers, especially Science and English. The science teacher looked like my mom. I also got along with the teachers at Fair View. Eventually, I was able to make some improvements in my life by developing new friendships. I got two new "friends," and their names were William and Victor. Let's start with William first. He was very intelligent and a straight-A student. Then through him, I meet Victor. He was a nice in the beginning but then treated me like trash. I had to deal with his attitude for the sake of keeping my friendship with William. He even hit me in fourth grade and bullied me until fifth grade. Worst of all, I was unable to defend myself, and it was here that I just began to blame my unknown disability. Despite this negative situation, in 2001 I was able to travel for the first time.

CHAPTER 6: FIRST TRIP TO FLORIDA

In the summer of 2001, I was able to travel out of Puerto Rico for the first time. I went to Florida, where my mom was living. In that trip, I went to places that I had never been before. I first went to the Islands of Adventures and Universal Studios. There, I rode the Jurassic Park ride and other amazing attractions. Then I went to Sea world, and it was here that I took the Atlantis ride, saw Shamu, and took the Wild Arctic Ride. Then I went to Busch Gardens. I rode some of the best roller coasters in the world, despite having a fear of rides at the same time. I also loved the zoo area of Busch Gardens. Then, I achieved one of my dreams of going to Disney world. First, I went to Epcot. The only thing that I liked here was getting into Spaceship Earth and the international atmosphere. Next, I went to the Magic Kingdom, where I fulfilled another dream of mine and took a picture with Mickey Mouse in person. Then finally, I went to MGM studios. I took the ride that I waited to take for a long time: Star Tours (Star Wars)! It was a 3D simulation ride. It took me through the entire SW universe and was super fun. This was an experience that I will never forget in my life. I even went to the Tattoine style shop next to Star Tours (where I got a cup made of ice, which lasted for years). Last, but not least, I went to the Animal Kingdom. The only thing I remember about the Animal Kingdom was the Bug's life attraction and Kali River Rapids. The last thing I did on the trip was to go to Cape Canaveral Space Station (NASA). Overall the trip was very good, and I had a great time. However, I didn't saw my mom in person for 2 years (until 2003). A year later in 2002, my younger sibling Paul was born.

MEETING MICKEY MOUSE

WITH MOM

CHAPTER 7: LIVING WITH FATHER

Now I am going to talk about the first years living with my father. It was weird living with my father when usually children live with the mother after a divorce. It was a time of confusion and difficulty. One highlight of these early years with father was when he planned my 11th birthday party in 2001. It was the biggest birthday celebration that I'd ever had and still is to this day. The main reason was that they also celebrated the birthdays of his best friends during the same day. Most family members came to the party. However, something strange happened to me that night. I went to the apartment to get another towel for the pool. Then when I got back to the elevator, I met a group of young drunk people. They were touching all the buttons of the elevator. I got scared, and I got out of the elevator and went down to the pool using the stairs. Despite this inconvenience, it was a great day.

Then we enter 2002. This year we moved to a bigger house in a neighborhood close to the condominium that we were previously living in. The good thing was that we were going to have more space since we were moving to a house. The bad thing was that the street was small and narrow, and the area was not good. The people in the neighborhood were annoying, so I went out less and less from my house. Looking back now, I should have ignored the annoying people and should have gone out more often and met the right people. Perhaps this would have made the difference with my challenges in life. This was part of the greatest struggle that I have had in my life and that unfortunately, I still have been unable to overcome to this day.

CHAPTER 8: FRIENDSHIP FAILURES

In 2002, I entered the sixth grade. It was there that I met my third new friend, Jose. We started the friendship by talking about video games. At the same time, I started to have problems with both William and Victor. They were treating me badly, and it got worse every day. Even worse, they pressured me to drop Jose and ignore him for no reason. This was a clear sign that those friendships were coming to an end. I should have found new people and tried to create better friendships. This was a struggle that I had to deal with.

It was during the sixth grade that I started to invite these people called "friends" to my house to play video games. We usually did it on Saturdays. We had good moments, but also bad moments when they complained when they lost games. Overall, it was a good initiative, which I would use over the next couple of years to invite other people. During my elementary school years, I always had excellent grades despite my difficulty building connections with the other students. I remember that during this time, I barely studied for the tests because the material wasn't too complicated, and it was easy to retain the information. This happened despite my disability. However, the bad thing about getting good grades was that it turned into an unhealthy obsession, which led me to be afraid of punishment if I didn't get good grades. I believe that my disability had to do with this obsession. Not to mention that I was also in an unhealthy competition with other students in terms of getting good and better grades than them. This lasted throughout my school life. This was made worse by William, as he always ridiculed me and was always bragging about having better grades than me. This contributed to ending that friendship. Even worse, I was not able to defend myself correctly against their bullying. Later in 2003, I was able to graduate from elementary school with a 3.97 GPA. I was frustrated that I did not have a 4.00 GPA due to the unhealthy habit and obsession of having all A's. Also in 2003, my older siblings graduated at the same time (Rachel graduating high school and Julian graduating middle school). In addition, mom visited Puerto Rico with my new brother Paul. We had a great time, and we went to different places. Overall, May 2003 was the only good month of that year. However, it was this year that the condition that I still suffered greatly for the next ten years began to present itself: clinical depression. During the sixth grade, I was in the process of applying to middle schools. I took different assessments to apply to some of the top middle schools in Puerto Rico (like Baldwin school and Colegio San Ignacio). However, I was unable to the get the results that I needed in order to get accepted into one of these schools (For Baldwin school, they were going to select only 2 students, and I finished in 4th place for their scholarship). After this, father used the results of Baldwin school to get me into Colegio Nuestra Señora de la Providencia, a Catholic school. The first time I heard about this school was from Jose. He was going to go to this school. Also, my father was considering putting me in other private schools such as Sagrado Corazones, Rosa Bell, and Colegio Marista. The issue that I had here that was affecting my life negatively was the tendency of not being alone. I made the erroneous assumption that I needed to go to a school which one of these "friends" was going to and because of this, I told dad to put me in Providencia, where Jose was going. Then, we had a meeting at Providencia with the school principal. After the meeting, father enrolled me at this school. It was done and like it is said in Spanish: "la suerte esta hechada." There was no turning back. This right here was the biggest mistake that I ever made in my life. Starting in 2003, I went through the most challenging period of my life.

WITH FATHER AT SIXTH GRADE GRADUATION

WITH MOTHER AND PAUL AT SIXTH GRADE GRADUATION

CLINICAL DEPRESSION AND DISCOVERY (2003-2007)

CHAPTER 9: MIDDLE SCHOOL

In August 2003, I started my first year at middle school. This was important because it set the tone for the four years of vicious bullying that I spent in this school. I was scared because I didn't know what to do. I introduced myself in front of my new classroom, and the bully attacks began immediately. It was unbelievable that on the very first day of school, my new classmates began to bully me. The only good thing was the home classroom teacher. That's it. I also like the History, English, and Math teacher. At the same time, I also had bad teachers during 7th grade. One teacher I had problems with was the religion teacher. She was arrogant, especially when one time she didn't let me enter the cafeteria because I supposedly out of line. However, strangely we had a cordial relationship after 7th grade. However, she wasn't as bad as the science teacher. I was really terrified to enter his classroom every day. He made me go through different humiliating events. I almost didn't pass his class. He affected my life in different aspects. Starting with him, I began to study more for all the classes and this continued up to college. This created an unhealthy habit of spending more time in the house studying, which made it more difficult for me to build social relationships. This contributed to my chronic depression. Despite studying a lot for his class, I had the grade of C no matter how hard I study. It was the only C for this course since I got A's in the other classes. The worst part of it all was that I would get the same science teacher for 10th grade. I talk about this later. In terms of the relationships with other students, I had Jose from elementary school as a friend, but we were not in the same classroom. In my own classroom, I didn't have a close connection with any student as they began to bully me immediately starting from the first day of school. They attacked me because I was not falling for their jokes. Also, in this grade, I began to receive homophobic attacks because I didn't fall for their tricks of being forced to like girls at the time. I was bullied more here than all my elementary school years combined. I thought that being enrolled in a private school would improve the situation, but it did the opposite. They made my life worse. They even told me that I was inhuman.

The classroom did so much damage to me that I had to start talking to the school psychologist to see if she could help me. This helped a little bit, but the attacks continued. Despite this situation, I was able to be somewhat successful and meet more people as "friends". In fact, I was able to build a closer connection to these people than with the former friends from elementary schools. The first one was Alejandro, who was a fellow Star Wars fan. Then I meet Pedro. He was serious, but at the same time, a good guy and an excellent student. I was able to meet other people, and I thought they were going to be friends, but I never had a good relationship with them. Therefore I was rejected by them. Similar to what I went through with William and Victor, I was forced to be with these people because they were friends with Alejandro and Pedro. Only Alejandro and Pedro were very close to what I consider to be friends. At the same time, my friendship with Jose decreased significantly, and we were no longer friends even though I enrolled in this school because he was going there too. Overall, my first year of middle school was a complete nightmare and as time went on it only grew worse. However, in 2004, an important event happened that would be critical for the rest of my life. It was the event where I found out what I truly had.

CHAPTER 10: THE DISCOVERY: AUTISM

My father took me to this event about this thing called "Autism". It was the first time I heard this word or term, "Autism." They told me that this is what I officially had and was diagnosed with. The real question was why I came to find out about Autism at this late stage of my life? My mom never told me about Autism when I was living with her. My father didn't tell me until that event. It wouldn't be until later that I found out that there were different forms of autism. I then proceeded to get more information and then a couple of years later my dad told me that I was diagnosed with a specific type of Autism called Asperger's Syndrome. I reviewed the information about the disability, and it said that people with Autism had different types of challenges based on their level of functioning. I saw parallels between the struggles I had and the challenges that people with Autism had such as verbal impairment, struggles in communication, and difficult building relationships with other people. This event was the beginning of learning more about my connection to Autism. Despite this, my life didn't improve when I did research about Autism, but I became more aware of the disability and how it impacted my life.

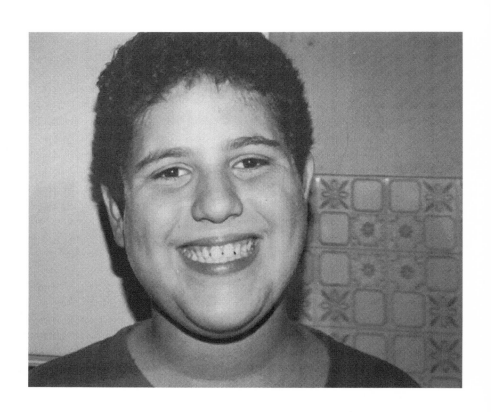

CHAPTER 11: DEALING WITH DEPRESSION

As we entered the end of 2004, my life challenges continued to increase. Not only was I dealing with my disability (now that I knew that I had Autism), but I was also dealing with severe clinical depression. I continued to get bullied at school, this time being in the worst classroom in 8th grade. Also, I ended my friendships with William and Victor that same year. They bullied me so much that it was time to end it. To deal with all of this negativity in life (bullying, depression, etc.), I got more attracted to video games and Star Wars. During those years, I enjoyed the Star Wars prequels. Despite this, it was not enough at all to deal with the negativity in my life. During the time between 2004 and 2007, I tried super hard to build real friendships. I was somewhat successful in which I was able to build connections with Pedro and Alejandro. Again, I tried everything to be their friend, but I was treated with rejection despite the fact that we were supposed to be in the same group of friends. However there were times in which I was also ignored not only by the other people in the group, but I was also rejected and ignored by Alejandro and Pedro from time to time. This was unnecessary, and it contributed to my depression. Despite this, I stayed friends with them because I didn't have anybody else to be with.

Because of their unnecessary behavior, I tried then to establish friendships with other people, but that didn't work either. The worst part of all was that I was unable to clearly understand them. This is one key symptom that I was able to identify about being on the Autism spectrum. They were a lot of things that I didn't understand from people, especially jokes. This could be one of the reasons why people thought I was weird, and as a result, I was bullied to no end. I tried my best to fit in with different groups but to no avail. Also, it is important to remember that I was also responsible for this, regardless of the disability. For example, one at the things that I dealt with were the demands of the people I hung out with not to be friends with other people because if I did, they wouldn't talk to me anymore. Instead of standing out for myself, I stayed in the comfort zone with the same people out of fear of being alone. This affected my ability to reach out to other people of different interests. For everything that I went through at this school, I was focused on finding a way to get out and go to a new school. I even tried to move to Florida and finish high school over there. However, because of problems that my mom was going through over there, it didn't happen. Despite these situations, I was able to survive and get good grades with a few exceptions at this school. I had a great relationship with my teachers, with the exception of a few. I liked the history teachers (all grades), music teacher, religion teacher (9th and 10th grade), math teacher (8th and 9th grade) and many more. I especially loved the piano class, and for a time I thought I was going to be a pianist. I also took art and computer classes. However, there were negative teachers such as the math teacher of 10th grade, who was very strict and yelled at me a lot. Then I took classes again with the same science teacher from 7th grade in 10th grade. It was tough but not as bad as the 7th grade. Also, I did my first communion in the 7th grade (usually done at the 3rd grade). Because of this inconvenience, I was embarrassed since I was older than the other students taking first communion classes, but regardless it was done. Overall, my experience with Providencia was pure survival, but it could have been handled better. I left this Catholic school in 2007, and I went to another Catholic school to finish the last two years of high school.

Despite going through so many schools and struggling with friendships from 2000 to 2007, I was somewhat able to make improvements in my verbal skills and was able to communicate more normally with people. Still, the communication and social relationship issues, even though somewhat improved, also continued to give me challenges in my life. Because of the issues that I was going through in my life, father got me to into psychiatry to see if my life could improve. The psychiatrists prescribed me Zoloft to help with the clinical depression that started in 2003, which was supposed to help me with my depression. It helped me initially, but it didn't make the difference in the end. In fact, it made my situation worse. What helped me during this time was playing video games (Xbox, PS2, GameCube, watching wrestling, and Star Wars). I played some of the greatest games during from 2003 to 2007, like Halo, Super Smash Bros, Star Wars Battlefront, WWE Smackdown series, Star Wars Knights of the Old Republic, and many more games. Without video games, my life would have been much worse.

THE SURVIVAL YEARS (2007-2011)

CHAPTER 12: WORSENING BULLYING

While 2003-2007 were very horrible years, the worst was yet to come. I left Providencia in 2007 and joined the Colegio Nuestra Señora del Rosario in Vega Baja, Puerto Rico in 2007 for the final two years of high school. The main reason why I went to this school was that my dad was going to get married again and that we needed to move to Vega Baja with his new wife and her kids. If I had a better experience in Providencia, perhaps I would have pressured my father to let me stay in Providencia. But the same can be said if I decided to go to another school. Also, my original plan was to go to Florida in 2007 and finish the last two years of HS living with mom, but it didn't materialize. Regardless, I saw this school as another chance to improve my negative life. In terms of the new household, even though I knew the people that I was going to live with for some time, they were still strangers to me at that time. There was no close connection during the time I was there, despite my efforts of building a better relationship.

My focus was to restart life at the new school, and I started living in Vega Baja, Puerto Rico in August 2007. I thought again that things were going to improve. But again and sadly, I was wrong. It was déjà vu again. Things started out well briefly, but again the attacks began. Imagine being in 11th grade and still being bullied. But the attacks were far worse than Providencia. I was viciously attacked so much that thoughts of suicide entered for the first time in a long time. I tried to fit in, but it was to no avail, it didn't work. The bullies of all schools had done so much damage, that the only way out for me was to kill myself. This is when for the first time I wrote my suicide letters. Despite this, I was unable to do it because of fear and lack of resolve. I felt powerless to do anything. The bullies' attacks came at the lowest point of my life. The bullies from all classrooms (10th and 11th grade) created two fake Myspace profiles. They stole my identity and wrote a lot of stuff that was simply not true. They said that I was homosexual and other horrendous stuff. The worse part was that I was unable to fight these criminals more aggressively. I tried to contact Myspace to shut down the fake profiles, but they didn't do anything about it. Looking back, I should have called the police and accused these bullies of ID theft. The bully attacks that have hunted me from all previous schools combined into this new school. The worst part of this history of bully attacks was that I was harsher on myself because I was unable to defend myself.

No matter what, I failed over and over again. My life at the new household was not getting better. My relationship with my siblings was nonexistent. I was left behind by other family relatives. I was attacked and misunderstood by everyone in the world. My "friends" from Providencia completely betrayed me and threw me under the bus. Even though I knew now that I had Asperger's, I still didn't know very much about the disability. I was wondering during this time why I just came to find out about Autism at this stage of my life and why my parents never told me about it. My father told me that I had Autism in 2004 and then later was confirmed that it was Asperger's Syndrome. My mom never knew about Autism, and they told her different things about what I had when she took me to different therapies during the 1990s. This is not uncommon. We heard cases of people not being told that they had Autism until later in life. It is a frustrating process for people with Autism to go through all these struggles. Being called retarded by adults and being insulted by bullies and misunderstood by everyone in this world for me felt like hell on earth.

With all the chaos that I was going through in my life, there was no escape to this nightmare. As a result, this was the first time that I wanted to get something and use it to kill to myself and end this nightmare, but I didn't do it and was not able to do. To be honest with you, I don't even know how I was able to survive those years.

During this time I tried to make new friends, and for a strange reason, I was somewhat more successful than the previous schools. In this new school, I was able to talk and find a connection with more people. That doesn't mean that I was successful here in creating real friendships. The first people that I met were Roberto, Saribet, and Ashley. They were nice and were excellent students. Later, I met Carlos and Daniel on a field trip to Ponce, Puerto Rico in 2007. We got hooked by common interests like Star Wars, video games, and other nerdy stuff. Then I was introduced to Peter by Daniel and Carlos. We didn't get along in the beginning, and we had some issues in 11th grade, but we

31

did improve our relationship, and he turned out to be one of the closest thing to a true friend.

Then I proceeded to meet Anton, Valeria, and Estefania. Anton was nice and a great gentleman. In fact, he was one of the very first people to actually come to me and introduce himself to me. Sadly, he left in the middle of 11th grade to another school. I wish I would have done more to stay in touch with him. I saw him as one of the potential future leaders of our time. Sadly, he passed away in September 2015. Estefania was very nice. In fact, she was the first student to ask me if I needed help in the new school and she told me to let her know. She was an excellent student. Also, I meet her cousin Valeria, and she was a nice person and an excellent student. Last, but not least, I meet Christian and he was in the other 11th-grade classroom. He was a nice person. We kept in contact after high school during college. We got to talk about things that happened later in my life (law of attraction, personal development, financial freedom, etc.). Despite the situation in the new school, however, in a strange turn of events, I was able to have more communication with more people here than I did from the previous schools. I was even able to talk to more girls than in the previous schools. Despite my disability and struggles with verbal and social communication, I was able to survive with no therapies and programs of support after second grade. I tried to talk to people as normally as I could, but they had no idea I had Autism. Eleventh grade was a bad year, but at the same time, was a learning experience. Not only was I able to expand my communication skills, but I became more approachable to people. Despite the struggles, I still was able to get excellent grades. I had great teachers like the history, Spanish and religion teachers. However, I had some mediocre teachers. For example, I had multiple English and Math teachers, which degraded the quality of the education for a private school and affected me severely as I went to college. However, something more important happened in 11th grade that affected me and continues to affect me to this very day.

CHAPTER 13: AN UNEXPECTED AFFECTION

One notorious event happened between late 2007 and early 2008 that also affected my life negatively. This started a bully attack, but it turned out to be more than that. When I was bullied, I was attacked for not liking a girl at the time. I was continuously pressured to like a girl during 11th and 12th grade. As I previously talked about it, this is the same line of attacks that I received in the middle school, in which I was bullied and accused of homosexuality. This is a situation in which I have struggled significantly and has affected my life super negatively. I didn't have what I called a female friend (the last time I'd had a friendship with a girl was in early elementary school). These girls from the bully group came to me to be their boyfriend as a joke and because of it, I refused to play along. All I was doing was being respectful, yet I was attacked because of it.

I really didn't know or understood the concept of girlfriends very much at all. I was bullied in school because I didn't say which girl I liked and because of it, I was called gay, homosexual or in the Spanish word "pato." They keep asking me which girls I like in public and due to fear of being beaten up by guys if I like a specific girl and also because of respect for girls, I didn't say it. However, then it came to a moment when I began to be asked if I like Estefania and Valeria. Here I struggled to answer, not saying no nor yes. But I had difficulty here: Not only were they excellent students, but also very beautiful girls. The difference here from the other girls that played jokes with me was that they had the whole package and I began to feel something for them. It first started with Estefania, but she already had a boyfriend. However, Valeria had never had a boyfriend. Everybody was trying to be her boyfriend. I didn't pay too much attention to it, but it grew more and more every day. I didn't know why. I hadn't even had a close relationship or friendship with a girl in a long time, probably never had one. I began to feel something for Valeria. This was bad and good. I began to be more pressured by classmates to like this girl. That eventually led to a series of embarrassing events such as writing a stupid diary sharing my feelings for her. I felt bad because I was embarrassing her. This led to a series of depression bouts, but for the first time in my life, I was dealing with the never ending struggle for a beautiful and nice girl. I told her about the situation, and she said that she wanted me as just a friend. But it didn't improve my situation. I invited her to my birthday. Never came. I wrote a poem for her; she rejected it. I was trying to stop this insane situation, and it led me deep into clinical depression. Then strangely she even erased me from social media. I was wondering why because I didn't do anything to her. It was such a depressive situation that I didn't even approach her during the prom. It was one of the worst moments of my life, and to this day it has haunted me because I left this unresolved. I followed the advice of the same people, and they said to forget about her, but it didn't help. This was just a sad situation that I was unable to go back and fix. In 2008, my clinical depression got worse and worse. I was in a breaking point having to continue to fail in my life day in and day out. However, in August 2008, I found a thing that perhaps finally might bring an answer to my problems. I thought that I found the key to getting and achieving my dream life. I discovered the secret: The Law of Attraction.

AT 11TH GRADE HONORS CEREMONY

PLAYING BASKETBALL

CHAPTER 14: THE LAW OF ATRACTION AND RELIGION

I watched the movie The Secret in 2008. I came away from watching it with the belief that I could use the Law of Attraction to have everything that I wanted, and I could have it if I believed it – that I would receive it like magic. However, this obsession failed when I didn't pass the SAT exam. I slid back into depression. I kept wondering why all of this is happening to me. Why me? Why go through this? Those are the questions that I still sometimes ask and still struggle to get answers to. The only thing positive again were my school grades.

Also, I struggle when selecting a major for college and I still failed at that. I would switch options, leading to too much indecision. I kept wondering when was all this going to end? WHEN?? I felt completely alone. What helped me somewhat during this time was always looking forward to a better future. Also, playing video games and watching Star Wars movies helped me too. One thing that I thought it helped me was going back to church in 2009 and give religion one more try. This was because I read this book called The Purpose Driven Way of Life by Rick Warren. I decided that all the problems in my life were happening because of me. That what I needed to do was to get closer to God in order to be saved.That year, I tried to do the sacrament of confirmation with the Catholic Church, but it never went through. After this, I left that church again. Then I began to go to different churches, but it didn't work and was wondering why. I tried my best to fit in, up to a point in which I became super religious. But at the same time, it didn't feel right. I felt that I was being dishonest with the creator. I thought that I had found the answer to my problems going to church, but it wasn't the case.

CHAPTER 15: COLLEGE ERA

I graduated high school in 2009, and I decided to stay in Puerto Rico for college. I was going to the University of Puerto Rico campus close to my house. The area I majored in was land surveying because it was something I felt I would "like" and would also offer me a high paying job. My Aunt Neida helped me in getting a land surveyor named Vicente Quiñones to be my mentor as a way to see whether there would be a fit for me as a land surveyor. This land surveyor was also a pastor, and it led me to go to one of his churches for a time.

In August 2009, I started my college career. I went to college because I was told that this would be the only way towards success. Later, it turned out to be inaccurate. The good thing about college was that there was no pressure from bullies as there was in school. I lost contact with people that I talked the most from middle and high school, even though they were not real friends. One reason why that connection ended was that they turned very negative and I needed to get out of those toxic "friendships." I tried to make new friends and connections in college. Despite the turmoil of the past, my focus was still to create a new life. I had some success in making connections, but new friends, not so much. The only connections that I remember that I made during my first college semester were Jose D and Hiram. Those were the closest connections I was able to have during my years in Puerto Rico. Ironically, I met them when I went to a Christian group in college. I met and had those connections because, during this time, I was in my super religious state. Both of them were excellent students and we got along pretty well. However, the issue that I had was that they were super religious. I tried to fit in over and over again, but it didn't really work. Despite this, I kept contact with them in those first two years. Besides this, I was almost completely alone during my college years in Puerto Rico. Even my grades started to go bad in my first semester of college. I finished the year with a 2.9 GPA. The most difficult classes that I had were chemistry, engineering, and pre-calculus. I studied for those classes, devoted more time and still was not getting the results that I wanted. This lead to more frustration in my life.

TRAINING TO BE A LAND SURVEYOR

AT DOWNTOWN DISNEY ORLANDO

CHAPTER 16: PERSONAL DEVELOPMENT

In 2010, I was still in the same rut. I wanted to get out of this nightmare. I was at the lowest point of my life and I had always wondered if it really was my fault or other people's fault. One positive aspect of the early months of 2010 was getting my driver's license. But unfortunately, I was not able to purchase an automobile due to lack of income and no support from anyone. I wouldn't get my first car until 2012. I was trying to survive as much as I could during this year. I had no friends left. My suicidal thoughts increased, and my depression worsened. There was no way to escape for me to save this life. I left religion full time and stopped going to the different churches. I was thinking that if I was not going to kill myself, then perhaps I should think about other alternatives, like joining the US armed forces, go to other countries, etc. I was thinking about all kinds of crazy scenarios to escape this depressive life. Because of the situation that I was going through, even my college studies were suffering.

With nothing to lose, I decided to give *The Secret*/ Law of Attraction one last opportunity. During the summer of 2010, I regained the strength to get back into this area, only this time it was more in depth. I officially entered the personal development world. I first started with reading and listening to Napoleon Hill (*Think and Grow Rich*). Then all of a sudden, a new light of hope was formed. There was hope that perhaps I can achieve a much better life. I was cautious because I didn't want to repeat the same mistakes of *The Secret* in 2008. Here I learned more in detail about the law of attraction, but now I was getting into the area of business and success. I started my personal development journey during my summer vacation in 2010. From Napoleon Hill to Jim Rohn, I studied their philosophies of achieving financial freedom and creating my dream life. I spent hours reading, listening, and watching material from Jim Rohn. The way he was talked and his message made a lot of sense. I finally was able to learn from someone that became a millionaire at a young age. Then, from him, I learned more about Tony Robbins and his teachings. From there I got into Robert Kiyosaki, author of the famous book *Rich Dad Poor Dad.* Then, I learned more about financial education and freedom. I began to think that there was more to life than just getting by with a job, going to school, and settling for mediocrity. I began to think that perhaps I could achieve financial freedom and become a millionaire or perhaps a billionaire.

Personal development, financial freedom, and goal setting help me alleviate the depression and circumstances that I was going through during the worst time of my life. The difference was that during this time, I was not going to give up like I did with *The Secret* in 2008. This time I was committed to accomplishing my dream life. I wrote my first complete list of goals in 2010, and I had huge dreams, e.g., becoming a millionaire and achieving financial freedom by the age of 26. Achieve the ultimate life and helping others who are in need. I thought that I had found the master key to success during my personal development journey in 2010-2011.

In this period, significant changes happened in all areas of life. I began to think that I was wasting time in college and that I needed to leave in order to accomplish my true dreams. That I needed to disassociate myself from losers and only be with the successful people. That everything was my fault and that I needed to assume complete responsibility for my actions. That I needed to think positively and watch out for anything negative, similar to what I heard in 2008 with *The Secret*. I began to really listen and watch a lot of stuff from the most successful people in the world. I read books like *Think and Grow Rich, Rich Dad Poor Dad, As A Man Thinketh, The Master Key System, The Science of Getting Rich*, etc. It was all self-help, personal development, and business material.

During 2010-2011, I was working to start my business in order to accomplish financial freedom. I first got in contact with network marketing. I thought that this was going to be a great way to start a business with low costs and low risks. However, at the same time, a part of me told me that the promises of network marketing of big income and having freedom were too good to be true. I went to an Amway conference in 2010, and it left me excited. However, I told my father about it, and he gave me the black eye. Then I researched Amway, and I got turned off immediately by the fact that it is a pyramid scheme and scam. This was one of the things that I tried in order to start my business in order to accomplish financial freedom for good. I had ideas of business, real estate, etc. However, there were not many results from it. The main issue here was that I was not taking real significant action towards accomplishing my goals. I thought that I was taking action, but again I was failing. My life was not truly changing. I was trying to be nice to everyone, not letting others control my life, but it was not working. I had no real friends at that point. I was making miracles to survive all of these challenges that I was going through. I tried and tried but no matter what, nothing was working. I thought that enough was enough and in late 2011, I decided that I needed urgently to leave Puerto Rico.

CHAPTER 17: LEAVING PUERTO RICO

I decided to move to Florida and live with mom because I had nowhere else to go. I had nothing left, so finally I made the decision to leave college for an indefinite period of time. Perhaps even drop out of college for as long as I was working towards accomplishing my true life. I felt this was way overdue and that I should have left Puerto Rico at least immediately after graduating High School. I first entered into land surveying and then I change majors to psychology. I thought that I was going to finish my bachelor's degree in psychology, but I was failing because of the clinical depression and the challenges being in the Autism spectrum. This severely affected my college studies. Despite this, I was able to complete the semester and bring my overall GPA to 3.5. I got the credits that would help me in transferring to another college in the USA if I were to go back to school. What should have been a period of goodbyes with friends and family was almost nonexistent. I left Puerto Rico with severe scars from a life full of struggles. I don't know what difference it would have made if I would have taken other actions in improving my life in all areas. What if I told others that I had Asperger's, would that have made them more understanding or would they have behaved much worse? I'll never know, but I do know that I should have left early and avoided the wasteful years of 2009-2011. This continues to have a negative effect on my life. I am grateful that my mom agreed to let me live with her. I didn't know what would happen next, but finally the day that I had waited for finally came.

On Tuesday, January 17, 2012, I finally left Puerto Rico to move to Florida. It was a day full of mixed emotions and regrets. But the past was done, and I was given a new chance to start a new life. There were just a couple of things that I was going to miss from Puerto Rico like the great culture, mountains, food, and some places like the Castillo Serralles. Overall, I left full of regret, hurt and defeated. But, now it was time to bury the past for good. I completely lost contact with the remaining connections from school and college life at that point. I tried everything to save the remaining friendships I had from high school and college, but they turned negative, and they were criticizing me nonstop. It was time to end those unhealthy "friendships." Overall, I tried everything I had to improve my environment, but no matter what, I failed. I thought that things were going to improve once I moved to Florida and in different aspects, it did. However, there were events that happened that shaped my life to where it is today. My life in Puerto Rico was over, and now my life in Florida began.

MOVING TO FLORIDA (2012-2015)

CHAPTER 18: LIFE RESTART

I moved to Florida in January 2012. I thought I had left school forever, but also a part of me thought that there was a chance that I go back to college. My focus was to use this new opportunity to start or restart my life. I needed to let go of the negative past and move on. The goal was to get into the marketplace and start getting the experience necessary to start my business and achieve my goals. However, so many things changed, and new challenges appeared. I moved in with my mom for the first time since 2000. So much had changed since then. Now I would be also be living with my younger sibling for the first time. Both of them were going through a lot in the last years before I arrived. I hoped that with me moving in that it would help to improve the situation. Good news is that I would have more freedom to do things since I was living in a very restrictive environment at father's house. The goal was to use the material learned from personal development and apply it towards achieving financial freedom. This time there would be no excuses. However, something was brewing that would nearly destroy my life.

CHAPTER 19: NEGATIVE OBSESSION

During this time, there were the negative habits returning from reading negative news. This started around 2003. I didn't know exactly why I became obsessed with the news, but, this obsession turned out to be very negative in my life. Because of this, I thought that all the negative circumstances were happening not because of me, but because of others. That my life was being determined by forces out of my control and that there was not much I can do to change it. I left this negative obsession in 2010 and went to focus on personal development, self-help, and financial freedom between 2010 and 2011. However, in late 2011, the negative obsession returned, and it followed me as I moved to Florida. For example, during the Sandy Hook Elementary School shooting in 2012, the media was saying that the shooter was diagnosed with Asperger's. This created a false connection between Autism and violence. When this was happening, I was letting the negativity of this situation control me and I was afraid that something may happen to me because there was this false image in the media that said that people with Autism are violent. This obsession with negative news leads me towards falling into this fear of life in an unhealthy way. I feel like I was derailed from my personal development journey. I don't know why I attracted this crap. Because of this, I feel that I was forced out of my real goals of life for the next four years. I feel depressed that my prime years were wasted on these fearful events that never happened. I feel that an injustice was done against me through this fear obsession, which stopped me from achieving my true life goals.

CHAPTER 20: FIRST JOB

Also, I was struggling in finding a job in order to provide income to support the household. My struggles with Autism in terms of verbal and social communications were not recovered completely. I was more a liability to mom and Paul's life than an asset. I realize now I can no longer blame others for my struggles in my life, regardless of having a disability. As a result, I started to take action in starting tasks and taking more responsibility in my life. First, I needed to get a job not only to get an income but most importantly to get into the marketplace for the first time. This would clear my mind in regards to starting a business and making investments. I tried to get help from Vocational Rehabilitation in my area to see if they could help me find a job since I was a person with a disability. I did initially receive some help, but they didn't help me at all in securing my first job.

After struggling in finding a job, I finally received a call for a job interview. The call was from the Home Depot store near home. I was worried that I was going to that interview with no support from VR. I wanted to make sure that my struggles with Autism and depression would not hold me back from getting a job. In April 2012, I went to the first job interview of my life. I was fighting anxiety, and it was a struggle when I was being asked difficult questions. Then I got more comfortable, and I learned to focus on how I could help the employer instead of what they could do for me. The interview was with one of the assistant managers at the store. Then I left the interview, thinking that I didn't do too well. Then I received a call for a second interview with the store manager. Then I went to the second interview, still dealing with anxiety, but more confident than the first interview. The second interview went smooth, and again I focused less on myself and more on how I could help the employer. At the end of the interview, the store manager offered me the position on the spot. Late, but I finally had a job. I worked for Home Depot as a cashier. I was finally earning income in the marketplace. Also, after trying to get my own vehicle in Puerto Rico, I was able to learn how to really drive a manual transmission. Even though it was scary and stressful at the beginning, I eventually was able to learn how to drive a manual transmission on the Honda Civic. I was able to purchase my first car in October 2012.

47

Finally, I was doing more independent things in my life. However, I was still struggling with making connections/ friends at work. At the same time, I was also struggling at the new job. Since this position was customer service, it meant that it was 100% interaction with people. As part of my condition, I struggled in being able to understand people effectively and efficiently in a high pressured multi-tasking environment. I needed to process transactions and payments, make change, while at the same time, provide service and communicate with the customer and co-workers. I struggle tremendously at first, and I thought that I would not be able to survive. However, instead of continuing to blame my disability and struggle again to find another job, I focused on not letting the disability determine what I could and could not do in my life. I continued to improve and focused on doing the very best I could at this job. I took the approach of doing more than what I was getting paid for and going beyond everybody's expectations. Despite the struggle with social communication, short-term working memory, anxiety and relationship building, I was able to survive in the job and was able to keep the job. Still, I was not happy at my job, with some co-workers not treating me well, dealing with rude customers and dealing with the difficulty of manual labor in this position. I felt that this job was not really helping me in getting the skills necessary to start my business at that time. I even got injured at the job lifting heavy concrete bags when I was dealing with an unstaffed store. Because of my challenge with customer service, I wanted to see if perhaps a job that required less social communication would be a better fit. Besides the job, getting independent skills and other things, an area that I continued to fail in was building new relationships. It was more of a challenge since I was out of the school/ college environment.

One positive highlight of 2012 was when I went to my first Star Wars convention! Star Wars Celebration VI was held at the Orange County Convention Center in Orlando, FL. It was a dream for me to be surrounded by Star Wars fans from all over the world. It was fun to go to all vendor booths and see the different toys and other items. Seeing people with different costumes was very fun too and even taking pictures with some of these people. Then I went to the first panel for the animated series The Clone Wars. It was pretty cool. But the biggest and at that time the greatest moment in my life happened at this panel. The person behind it all appeared live in front of my teary eyes. I finally saw the creator of Star Wars in person: George Lucas!! I got super excited and was crying like a little kid, full of enjoyment. Despite leaving the day early and things not going exactly as planned, this was a day I will never forget.

Overall, I was depressed that I was not making enough progress. I was now doing what should have been done years ago in Puerto Rico. I was severely behind. Now, I was blaming myself for the struggles that I was going through. My low esteem continued to affect me as we entered 2013, a year that my life almost ended.

CHAPTER 21: THE ALMOST END

As of 2013, I was struggling in all areas of life with nothing positive coming. Being mocked by blood relatives and former so-called friends about leaving school and working a minimum wage job. No new friends and struggles with social communication. Depression at the highest level. Everything was going wrong. I felt like I was a waste in this life and that no matter what I did, I was failing. During this year, I struggled and continued to struggle. I attempted to do other things to escape my situation. For example, after struggling with social communication and multitasking at Home Depot, I got a full-time job at a hotel as a housekeeper aide. I thought that since this job required less social communication and less dealing with customers that I was going to thrive in this environment. However, I ended up being wrong. The environment was not good. The person who trained me for the position wanted to get rid of me because she wanted to put her friend in the same position. My struggles with Autism made me unable to respond to these cases against me more effectively. Not to mention that the job was more manual labor, minimum wage, and I worked almost 7 days a week. This contributed to the worsening condition of my depression, and I tried to find ways to end my life during the summer of 2013, just like I tried to commit suicide in Puerto Rico when I was living a worse situation. I was at the lowest point of my life. I was a burden, and I felt that I needed to be eliminated so a better world could rise. I don't know how I am still alive after going through clinical depression for more than 10 years. There was something that stopped me from going ahead with these suicidal plans. I don't know what it was, but something wanted me to stay alive, while another wanted me dead. I thought that nobody liked me and that I was a negative force in the world. The job at the hotel was making things worse with my condition. I needed to find something to escape again or to solve the problem. Then, out of complete desperation, I decided that I would go back to college.

CHAPTER 22: RETURN TO COLLEGE

I had not expected to go back to college, not that soon. I took the credits that I had from Puerto Rico to transfer (since I was not going back to Puerto Rico to finish college), and I applied to Seminole State College of Florida. They had an associate in science degree program in Entrepreneurship, as this is what I was going to do because of my business goals. I had struggled with the admission application process and barely passed the exam to not take English again in college. But passing the test helped me in getting accepted to Seminole State College in August 2013. Now I had the goal of being in college and completing an Associate's degree in Entrepreneurship. Initially, I felt like a loser going back to school. However, I saw this as a new opportunity to get the tools and knowledge necessary to start my own business. I thought that this would be my last chance to start new friendships and connections. By this time, all the connections and people from the previous school life were gone.

I did well during my first semester back in college, getting all A+'s. I took classes that would help me with a business like introduction to business, public speaking, Microsoft Office applications, and business communications. Now I was taking classes that I really wanted to take. Also, I liked the campus and the way it was structured. For some strange reason, it felt good being back in college for the first time in my life. There was a minor issue that almost got me to leave college again, and it was of not having enough financial aid for the next semester and beyond. This happened because I spent the first two years of college in Puerto Rico and I had a lot of credits when I came to Seminole State. However, my student advisor Maritza helped me in fixing the issue, and she worked out a plan that put me on a path towards first getting my Associate in Business degree in May 2014 and then going straight to the bachelor's degree in Business and Information Management. So the problem of financial aid was fixed for the moment.

I ended 2013 with me being back in school, but I had survived one of the most challenging years of my life. This is one of the worst years alongside 2003-2011. I had no job once again, was broke and depressed with no social life, and I was still trying to figure out what I came here to do. That is what I was fighting with every day. 2013 was one of the worst years of my life and now here comes 2014. In my second semester of school, I took 5 classes, more than the first semester. It was because of the requirements of graduating with my associate's degree, which would be used to get into the Bachelor's degree in Business and Information Management. I took more difficult classes like macroeconomics, statistics, and financial accounting. I also took History of USA and English II. I had the most challenge with statistics, struggling with different formulas. This took me back to pre-calculus during my first time in college. I even got an F for the first exam; I was stressed out with anxiety, trying to figure out how I would be able to survive this course. Eventually, I was able to learn to use the statistical programs and graphics calculator and was able to pass the class with an A. The other difficult course was Macro-Economics, but it was more for the assessments. Eventually, I was able to pass the course. But the most important and also challenging class was the financial accounting course. I learned a lot about financial statements and other material like balance sheets, accounts payable and budgets. Financial accounting felt like a course that I was really going to need it for business and it was. The professor was Terri Walsh, and she helped me a lot during this class. I was able to learn a lot of accounting, and I credit her for it to this day.

Not only accounting, but she also taught me how to do networking with other people. This was the critical area that I was struggling with throughout my life. I was able to go to networking events and other events through the Accounting Club. The first networking event that I went to was a business etiquette dinner. I was seated at a table with other students and two business leaders. I spoke with these leaders in regards to career options and how to be successful in the marketplace. Going to these events helped me a lot. In fact, because of these networking events, I ordered my own business cards. I had come to network events with resumes, but I learned it was more fitting to bring business cards and be able to make connections with other people in business. This also helped me to improve my social and communication skills, despite the big challenges with Autism. I was not successful most of the time, but this helped me significantly in improving my communications with other people not only in business but also life in general.

In 2014, things began to improve a little bit in my life for the first time. I got a part-time job as a federal work study at school. I was able to make life improvements during this first half of 2014. The negative news obsession that had control of my life for the last couple of years was diminishing. Also, I went to my first March Madness (college basketball) game in March 2014. It was a great basketball game, and it was a good time with my younger brother Paul. Then a very important moment came. After finishing the spring semester with all A's, I graduated with my Associate's degree in Business on May 4, 2014. Even though it was an associate degree, it was an important accomplishment. I felt that finally, I was able to accomplish something important in life. To all the people that were saying that I would never to go back to college, I proved them wrong. For me, it felt and it began to grow on me that I truly had the capacity and capability to accomplish great things in life. This was one of the most important weekends of my life. Friday, May 2, 2014, was the business etiquette dinner where I was able to learn how to network and build business relationships. Sunday, May 4, 2014· was the graduation ceremony from Seminole State College, in which I got my associate degree. But, on Saturday, May 3, 2014, I volunteered at the Autism Walk and Family Fun Event day, organized by the Autism Society of Greater Orlando. This was the beginning of an important stage of my life.

WITH MOM AT THE GRADUATION FOR ASSOCIATE'S DEGREE

CHAPTER 23: AUTISM ADVOCACY

Saturday, May 3, 2014, was the day that I officially started my Autism advocacy, which would be and is still is my greatest achievement in life. For a long time, I have thought about doing something or volunteer in an Autism/ Asperger's related event. I always talked about it, but was unable to do so and also didn't try hard enough in finding opportunities to do something to help the Autism community. Then after being in Florida for two years, I finally saw the opportunity to volunteer at an Autism event. That day on the Autism walk, I volunteered at the entrance greeting participants and checking their wristbands. Before this, I have done volunteer work in Puerto Rico. I volunteered with the organization "Para La Naturaleza of Puerto Rico" at their annual fair from 2009-2011. This opportunity was given to me by my aunt Neida, who worked with the organization. In these events, I was at the registration desk, helping register participants for the annual fair. I was able to greet people and also help with other tasks. Besides the volunteer/ apprenticeship experience I had with land surveyor Vicente Quinones, this was my other work experience in Puerto Rico. Being at the Autism walk and seeing families with loved ones with Autism, I felt like I was at home. It really didn't feel like work. Being able to greet between 2,000 and 3,000 participants at the entrance was something I will never forget. Here I was able to meet Donna Lorman, President of the Autism Society of Greater Orlando. What impressed me the most was that the people that were in leadership positions at this organization all of them had a family member with Autism. This is the day that I formed a connection to the organization, which led me towards playing different roles within the organization in the years ahead.

AT THE AUTISM SOCIETY OF GREATER ORLANDO AWARDS CEREMONY (2017)

CHAPTER 24: JOB STRUGGLES

One thing that happened a couple of months later was that I got officially back into the marketplace. Before the start of my college semester (Fall 2014 term), I got a part-time job with Sam's Club. I wanted to see if I could work part-time, while also going to school at the same time. I went back to retail because I was not able to find other options. I was hoping to get a bank or an administrative position at the time. But at least I was getting an income again. I wanted to give retail a second chance after my time with Home Depot. Starting at Sam's Club, I was hired as a cashier and the environment was familiar, but at the same time different. I struggled with social communication and working in a fast-paced multitasking environment. I was able to do my cashier duties well and went beyond expectations in providing excellent service to members despite my disability. However, the difference from Home Depot was that the position was more sales driven than customer service. In this position, I had daily quotas, and I had to sell three products: new plus membership signups, credit cards, and member renewals. I had to sell these programs, while at the same time doing cashier duties and providing excellent service. It was a struggle to multitask between these tasks. Not to mention that I was dealing with short-term memory issues and was struggling to explain the products to the customers in an effective and efficient way. I was coached several times at the beginning in terms of improving my sales skills. This was putting a lot of pressure on me. I didn't want to let my disability determine what I can and can't do. However, at the same time, I didn't want to be in an environment in which there was a lot of pressure about sales and multitasking. I was frustrated with myself in regards to not being able to get other types of jobs and that I needed to accept these jobs because I didn't have income. I didn't want to give up easily and let Autism control my life. I focused on improving and doing the best I can that I know that I am capable of improving my sales skills. After a lot of training, eventually I got comfortable with my sales pitch for the products, and I was talking with the members, while at the same time providing excellent service. Still, I was getting a lot of rejection and not hitting my quotas. This was when I learned that instead of just accepting no, I focused on building relationships with members. I focused on how the products could help improve the lives of the customers instead of the benefit to the store. Eventually, I was able to improve my relationship building skills, and

I was able to meet and exceed my quotas on a daily basis. There was a time when I was the associate that got the most plus memberships in the store for two straight weeks during the holiday season. Because of this, I was promoted to the member service associate position. It was a challenge every day in dealing with a multitasking and customer service/ sales environment. Still, I wanted to make sure that I was able to do the very best I was capable of doing and exceed expectations. Most of the coworkers were very good with me. There were one or two exceptions, one of them being my supervisor. She pressured me too much and was not very supportive when I needed help. As a person with Autism, I was unable to deal with this effectively and efficiently. I was too tired of this type of environment. But I will talk about this in a little bit.

At the same time I was working, I was starting my second year at Seminole State College, this time in the bachelor's degree program in Business and Information Management. I took 12 credits and enrolled in the following courses: Managerial Accounting, Microeconomics, Excel and Writing for Business. My favorite course was managerial accounting with Prof. Walsh. The most challenging was Microeconomics. I was able to learn to use Excel more effectively and efficiently and was able to improve communication and writing skills in the Writing for Business course. For this term, I was able to get excellent grades. I was handling going to school and working very well during my fall 2014 term. Despite these successes, I was still struggling with the clinical depression. During this year, I got more into playing video games again because of my depression. I played and purchased back classic consoles like the original XBOX, Super Nintendo, and Nintendo 64 in 2013. I also played NBA 2K14 a lot during 2014. I had this as a hobby during this time.

Unfortunately, this ruined my life a little bit since I was unable to truly learn the hobbies or build the habits necessary that would help me to accomplish a better life. However, in 2014, for the first time in a long time, I was able to make improvements in my life. During this year, I was able to learn the skills that would help me down the road in regards to accomplishing my life goals.

In 2015, I saw a lot of important events both good and bad. For the spring 2015 college term, I took more courses deep into the degree program. Finally, I took the Entrepreneurship course, in which, I wrote my first business plan. I also took strategies of Human Resources, which helped me get into one of the most important areas of business. Then I took History of Business, which I took with Prof. Tom Walker, who would later play a key role in my life. Last, but not least, I took Information systems. This semester was unique in my life in general. I was able to learn more about the skills required to start a business. Not to mention that I was able to get excellent grades during this semester. In terms of employment, I was still employed by Sam's Club in early 2015. Since I was tired of retail in general and struggling in this position, I wanted to see if I could get into banking. Again struggling with keeping a job, I read an article from Dr. Temple Grandin about what jobs are good and not good for people with Autism. The jobs that I had done, with the exception of education and hospitality, were jobs not recommended for people with Autism. No matter what I did, I still struggled in these jobs. I was struggling to find the best situation to succeed. I will talk about what happened with the job search later.

CHAPTER 25: BEST WEEK EVER!

One important event happened in April 2015. For the first time in my life, I went traveling solo to California for a whole week. The main reason for this trip was simple: Star Wars Celebration 2015!! This would be my second Star Wars Celebration, but it would be the first one in which I would be able to go all four days of the convention. Also, it was the first Star Wars celebration since Disney purchased Lucasfilm in 2012. I was super excited because they were going to talk about the new Star Wars movie, which was scheduled to be released in December 2015. Not only was I going to Star Wars Celebration, but of course, I was also going to different places in Southern California. The trip happened between April 13 and April 20, 2015. I traveled on Monday, April 13, 2015 to go to California. I arrived in Santa Ana, California. The next day, early, I went to Disneyland for the first time. I was able to go to many great attractions, especially Star Tours. Then I went to the Disney's California Adventure theme park. Even though it was a smaller park than Disneyland, it still was a lot of fun with great rides. Later that same day in the afternoon, I went to some of the best beaches in Orange County: Huntington Beach and Newport Beach. I was able to see some of the best scenery in my life. But my day was not done. Later that night, I went back to Disneyland and California Adventures. At night, I went on some of the rides I couldn't get on earlier during the day. But, I was so tired that at the end of the day I left the park as they were doing their fireworks show. Literally, I was pulling out of the parking lot as the fireworks were happening. It was a very long, but very fun day. The next not one, but two days would be the longest, but at same time, greatest days of my life.

On the third day, I drove early to Los Angeles. First thing I did was to go to the Griffith Observatory Tower. Here, I was able to get a spectacular view of Hollywood and the Los Angeles area. Then I went to Hollywood. First, I drove down Hollywood Boulevard and proceeded to walk along the Walk of Fame. While I was walking, I was also able to see Grauman's Chinese Theater in Hollywood. After this, I took a bus tour through Beverly Hills. During the tour, I was able to see the big houses and mansions of famous celebrities (Michael Jackson, Harrison Ford, etc.). It was very surreal for me to go to these places live and in person. After Beverly Hills, I went to Santa Monica Beach. Here I saw another spectacular view, and the pier view was amazing. After enjoying my time in Santa Monica Pier, I then went to an event that I had also been waiting for: go to a Lakers game at Staples Center! It was surreal being at the same arena that many legends of the game had played and obviously my favorite player of all time, Kobe Bryant. I was looking forward to seeing him play, but he was injured. I was not able to see him in person. Despite this, it was awesome to experience the great atmosphere at Staples. Even though my Lakers lost, it was still awesome to be there. This third day was a long one, full of events and activities (LA, Hollywood, Beverly Hills, Santa Monica, Lakers game, etc.). However, it was just the beginning.

At the same time that I was on the Lakers game, the line was already filling up for the start of the first day of Star Wars Celebration 2015. I left Staples Center and went to the hotel to get a quick shower. Then immediately changed my clothing and put on my Imperial Officer uniform and went immediately to the Anaheim Convention Center and waited in line for the first panel of Star Wars Celebration. I slept on concrete for hours, but at the same time, was super excited for the Star Wars Celebration. I slept overnight at the Convention Center. It was fun to meet Star Wars fans from all over the world at the same place and time. Then the fourth day of my trip arrived, and I went to the first panel for the new movie *Star Wars: Force Awakens*! It was very surreal that I was witnessing history in person for the Star Wars franchise. I saw JJ Abrams (Director) and Kathleen Kennedy (President of Lucasfilm). And finally, I saw some of the new actors of the movie and also the actors from the original and prequel trilogy! It was awesome to be at the same place and the same time as my idols from childhood. It was awesome to see images and footage from the new Star Wars movie. But the big highlight came when they released the second teaser of *The Force Awakens*. It was amazing being with my fellow Star Wars fans watching the teaser trailer. Then the entire arena got very emotional as we saw Han Solo and Chewbacca on the big screen for the first time in decades. People (including myself) were crying with joy living through this historic moment. After the panel, my adventure at Star Wars Celebration Anaheim went into full steam! There was so much to do on the exhibit floor from books, costumes, autographs, other panels, etc. It was going to be impossible to do it all. I was so overwhelmed that I was unable to do everything I wanted to do. One thing that I failed to do and was the reason I came here was to build new friendships with the Star Wars community. I was able to talk to Star Wars fans during the convention. However, my struggles with anxiety and disability didn't let me able to build new friendships. This is my frustration and no matter what I do; I continue to struggle in building new friendships, even with fellow Star Wars fans. Despite this, I was able to have a great time, and I was in my own world. Over the next couple of days, I did so many things. I got autographs and pictures with actors and actresses from the Star Wars universe: Mark Hamill, Carrie Fisher, Ian MacDiarmid, Billy Dee Williams, Kenny Baker and many more. Also, I went to panels, got new toys, and went to the Rancho Obi-Wan Exhibit. In here, I saw all types of costumes. Also, I saw the Star Wars movies on the big screen. I did so much stuff during the four days at the convention that I could keep talking about it for a long time. Overall, it was a magical experience being at the Star Wars Celebration 2015 for all four days!! To end the greatest week of my life, I was able to explore the mysterious and strange murals at the Denver International Airport during the final day of the trip. It was surreal being able to see these murals in person. With this, I concluded my trip to California/ Colorado in the spring of 2015. I was concerned before the trip in terms of how I was going to deal with the concerns of traveling by myself and being alone in different places, especially dealing with the challenges of Autism. Despite the challenges, I was able to handle those situations very well. This trip made me realize that perhaps I could accomplish greater things in my life. I may not have realized at the time and immediately, but this event led me towards getting back into the personal development world in 2016. I realized I could achieve greater things in my life. To this very day, the week of April 13-20, 2015, remains the greatest week of my life.

IN HOLLYWOOD!

WITH R2D2!

CHECKING WITH THE SCOUT TROOPERS ON LOCATING THE REBELS!

WITH JEDI MASTER HIMSELF, MARK HAMILL!

WITH PRINCESS LEIA HERSELF, THE WONDERFUL LATE CARRIE FISHER!

CHAPTER 26: SETBACKS AND DISCRIMINATION

I got back from my dream trip and returned to the same daily routine. Back to the struggles that I was having in all areas of my life. I was struggling in my job so much that I was looking for something else out of desperation. This has been the story of my work experience. It was then that I needed to look for a job that wouldn't involve too many issues with my disability. So I read the article by Temple Grandin again where she talked about the jobs that are good and not good for people on the spectrum. Bank teller position was on the list of jobs good for people in the spectrum. Cashier was on the list of jobs not recommended for people in the spectrum. Based on this list, I decided to look for banking jobs and get out of retail. Three months after coming back from California, on July 2015, I was offered a teller position with a local credit union. I was transferring now from retail to banking. One of the main drawbacks of the teller position was that it was a full-time position and at the same time I was going to school full time. I don't know how I was going to deal with it, but I was going to make it work somehow. I thought that finally I was in an environment that I could perhaps finally triumph and succeed. I thought that perhaps I was going to get much closer towards accomplishing my goal. However, as we enter the second half of 2015, this job would be the beginning of a situation that to this day continues to affect me in a negative way.

When I was hired at this bank, I was excited to get out of retail, and I thought that I found the job that I can work at and build my career. Training was good, but when I got into the branch, things got significantly worse. I struggled first with my short-term working memory in dealing with transactions and learning to use the systems effectively and efficiently. I was dealing with more money here. This was not what I expected for a job that was supposed to be good for people with Autism. I was focused on providing excellent service and doing the best I could and was able to receive good feedback from customers. However, the management team was not supportive from the beginning. In fact, they were overly critical. They were criticizing me for everything I did. It is fine to be criticized when job performance is not working and work on a plan to solve the problem. I have no issue with that. However, when my work ethic is being questioned and they say things that are not true, then this an example of a toxic work environment. I tried to follow everything they said. It was unacceptable to be criticized strongly since I had been with the company for a couple of weeks and still was in training. I felt that I was attacked and that I needed to explain why I was struggling. Then, they asked me if I had something wrong that was affecting my work. Once they asked me if I had something wrong, then I had no choice but to inform them about my disability. This was a red flag, and it meant that this job was coming to a quick end and that I needed to leave ASAP and find something else. But instead, I continued to give this job a chance. I didn't want to run and hide. They asked me for information about the disability, and I gave them information as requested. This was done to make "accommodations" for the job. I was not expecting any accommodation (which eventually they didn't do any accommodation). Instead, what they did was to give me a one week plan. I followed through very closely and did what they asked in order to do a better job. Providing great service, processing transactions effectively and efficiently, doing what I was told.

I thought that I did well in that week and that everything was going to be fine. Then a week later after working on the week plan, I was unexpectedly fired. For some minor mistakes and other things that they said happened and were not true, I was fired. This happened immediately after I informed them about my disability for the main purpose of doing accommodations as requested. The branch that I was working in was understaffed. They were "concerned" about my ability to do the job and that they didn't trust me at all. I was in a no-win situation. This led to more clinical depression and low self-esteem. How could it be that no matter how hard I worked at a job, I was still treated with disrespect and fired like trash? This was the first time that I was forced to inform an employer about my disability at a job. In my previous jobs, this was not necessary, and they never asked me anything about my disability. This was a stupid decision, and it was totally uncalled for. I was traumatized and stressed as to why I was fired. I was on time doing the best I could in the job. But, no matter what, I was always in a toxic environment. Since the incident and this job at a bank, my job situation was worse. I tried to file a discrimination lawsuit based on ADA (American with Disabilities Act). But since I was terminated during the 90-day probation period, I was unable to do so.

Now I was unemployed and since I recently left Sam's Club, I didn't have an income. One good thing about this misfortune was that perhaps staying at this job would have affected my grades negatively and since I was not working here, now I could completely focus on finishing school and getting my degree. After I was fired from this job, I was very hard on myself for how the situation ended, even though there were things out of my control. It was my focus on getting a part-time job for the time being to help me finish my degree. I only have one year left to complete my degree. Not to mention the fact that I didn't have a lot of financial aid left. Because of this, I needed to complete my bachelor's degree by December 2016.

A couple of months later, I was offered by the Autism Society of Greater Orlando to be part of the board of directors starting from October 2015. It would be the first time a person with Autism would be on the board of directors of the organization. This was an important step in continuing my volunteer work in the Autism community. The firing at the bank affected me in all areas of life. The last months of 2015 and early 2016 would be some of the worst months of my life. This time, however, it would lead me closer to getting back into personal development and achieving a great life down the road. During late 2015 and early 2016, me, mom, and Paul were very much challenged. Our lease was not going to be renewed at the rental house we were living, and we would need to find a new place to live. This was very challenging because we were struggling to find a new place to live. We submitted one apartment application after another and still nothing came of it. Our stress and anxiety levels increased as the date that we needed to vacate the house got closer. It was so bad that I was deeply worried that we were going to end up on the street and homeless. We didn't have anybody else to help us. I was wondering and questioning why this was happening. I personally didn't care what happened with me, but I was more concerned about what would happen to mom and younger brother. The situation was made worse because I didn't have any income. I got a part-time job at a call center in January 2016. I informed the apartment about the new job. A couple of days later the application to the apartment was declined because the new employer told them that it was a full-time job (this was an income restricted apartment community). Because of the emergency situation, I ended up leaving that job after I was there for only two days. It was one of the worst experiences of my life. I didn't know what else to do. Fortunately, a couple of weeks later, our application was reviewed and then approved.

Thankfully, we were able to move to the new apartment. It was a huge relief, but I still felt terrible because we went through this mess because of me. I was blaming myself nonstop since blaming others for my life struggles was not working. Despite going through these situations, this time I made a commitment to myself that I was not going to give up. I felt that instead of going deep into darkness, I was closer to accomplish my goals. That there was a light at the end of the tunnel and that it was time to keep moving and get closer to the finish line. It was time to complete my bachelor's degree and achieve victory in my life.

THE COMEBACK (2016)

CHAPTER 27: GETTING BACK UP

In 2016, I started the last year of college. I got excellent grades in the Fall 2015 term. One of the important classes that I took during this Fall 2015 term was marketing, which is a crucial skill in business alongside sales. Now for the spring 2016 term, I enrolled in the following classes: Selling and Negotiations, Principles of Finances, Information Systems and Enterprise Process. Finance was very difficult and was not able to learn much; however, I barely got an A+. Selling and Negotiation was very tough, but this class turned out to be the most important. Even though I got a B, I was not unhappy with the professor, because he taught me more about improving my sales skills regardless of the grade. This is without a doubt the most important class of the degree program. I didn't have the grades that I was hoping for due to the circumstances of moving to a new apartment, but I was able to survive the 2016 spring term with good grades.

One important event happened during April 2016. After being with no income, I accepted an offer from Prof. Tom Walker to be the Federal Work-Study for the business department. It would be a more administrative role than when I did Federal Work-Study back in 2014. I am grateful to him for giving me this opportunity.

My focus now was to complete my bachelor's degree before December 2016. If not, I would lose financial aid, which would cause me to not have the resources to go to college for another semester. Because of the situation, I needed to take classes over the summer 2016 term. I enrolled in Simulation, Project Management, and International Business. Taking Simulation and Project Management courses at the same time was going to be very challenging. However, I was focused on not letting doubt take over me. My focus was to complete these courses, so that way I could take my Capstone in Fall 2016. It was going to be a challenge, but it had to be done. While I was going to school and now doing Federal Work-Study, I was also volunteering with Autism Society of Greater Orlando on the board of directors. I was thankful for the opportunity to help the organization, and it was my responsibility to get support for the organization as a board member. This was the first time that I was also able to see the inner workings of a nonprofit organization. One of my main tasks for the 2016 Autism Walk was to follow up and get approval for the Wal-Mart Foundation grants. I called almost all the Wal-Mart and Sam's Club stores in Central Florida. I even went in person to a lot of Wal-Mart and Sam's Club stores in an effort of getting corporate sponsorships for the walk. Because of the effort, I was able to improve my sales skills. Despite sales being a very tough job for people in the ASD spectrum, I was doing what I could in making the connections to get support for the organization. Because of the effort, I was able to successfully get support from the Wal-Mart Foundation for the Autism Walk. It was a tough and difficult process, but it was done. Besides fundraising, I volunteered at as many events despite my schedule with work and school. Because of this, I felt like I wasn't doing enough to help the organization and make a big difference in the community. I wish I would have done much more. Still, I am proud of what I was able to accomplish in helping make the difference in the community.

Now, we go to the summer 2016 term. Simulation for me was one of the top classes of the program. My initial concern was that it required a lot of statistics. However, I was able to do well, and I had no issues using the software program called Arena. This program was used to create business process models. I was able to learn a lot from Prof. Richard Calloway. Despite being only six weeks of a high-intensity class, I was able to survive, and I got a good grade. Project Management was challenging because of the workload and the group project. Overall, it was very good, and the international business class was interesting because I was able to learn about how other countries did business. Overall, I was able to pass all the classes, and now I was ready for the final semester of college. I had mixed emotions because of all that I have gone through and what I was currently going through up to that point. I still didn't know what was going to happen after graduating from college, but my focus now was to finish and get the degree.

CHAPTER 28: PERSONAL DEVELOPMENT RETURN

During the summer of 2016, a more important development happened. Because of the frustration and failure that I had throughout my life so far, I decided one day to read the book Retire at age 26 by Asha Tyson. This is a book I had heard about when I was in personal development mode from 2010 to 2011, but I never read it. Now in 2016, I decided to give personal development a new chance. Once I finished reading the book, I proceeded to read the original version of the Law of Success by Napoleon Hill. I read the 1928 version in 2011, so it was interesting in reading the 1925 version in 2016. The book made more sense than the edited version, and from here I was able to learn more about accomplishing my goals and achieving financial freedom. Getting back into personal development was a very depressive experience. I had wasted years, especially the prime years of my life during the time which I went through the worst depression of my life. Now, we were in 2016, and I was still broken in all areas of life. I was focusing too much on my biological age and as to whether it was too late to accomplish the ultimate dream life. I was feeling very down when I was getting back into personal development. Originally, I had the goal of becoming a millionaire and achieved financial freedom at the age of 26, but I was at that same age still struggling with life. The area I was still struggling the most with was building relationships with other people. Despite this, my focus now was to start again with my goals, but the difference from 2010-2011 was that this time the focus would be to take real and massive action towards finally accomplishing my life goals. Not just read books and invest more in programs, but to really implement the information that I learned in order to achieve my true goals. I was focused on completing school and getting a job. Even though I didn't have my own business at the moment in summer 2016, my focus was to improve what I was learning so I could accomplish my goals. I was tired of all the setbacks in my life. My goal was to restart my life and be able to make a big difference in the World.

CHAPTER 29: ROADBLOCKS

Now, we are in the final semester of college: Fall 2016 term. For this semester, I was taking the following classes: Business Law, Business Processes, Operations Management and the most important, Capstone. The other class I was able to learn from was from Business Law, which is important if you are running your own business. It is important to be very familiar with local, state, and federal laws and regulations. But the pass or fail degree course of the entire program was Capstone. The real challenge was not who was going to be the client, but how I was going to form a team of students and be in the right situation to complete the project and pass the class. Group projects have been one of my biggest struggles in not only school but life in general. In school, I was always doing the most work and also I was disrespected because I struggled in social communication with people. I had a couple of group projects in college, and it was always the same story. For Capstone, the mission was to get the right people and in the right situation. Capstone was a group project for the entire semester. I had struggled during the group projects of Project Management and Simulation. For the simulation, I ended up doing most of the project. I can understand this being that this was a short-term class. For the project management group project, two students named Hiba and Dina from my Simulation work group came back. Besides these students, I had another student name Maria from the simulation class and Adam, whom I took managerial accounting with in 2014. I worked with Adam before on group projects in the past, and I have a good idea of what he could do for the group. I didn't know Maria very well, but she was friends with Hiba and Dina, so I accepted their recommendation to bring her into the group. One thing that I was impressed with was that she had extensive work experience and she eventually did a lot of work for the Project Management project. The issue with the project was that I was not also able to lead clearly with all participants of the group. The challenges continued during the Capstone final project. For Capstone, there was another student that came to the group named Marie, which came with a lot of work and leadership experience. In Capstone, there were issues of lack of communication and effort from some members of the group. I understood that some students were going through different circumstances like working a full time job, dealing with other classes, etc. A lot of times, again I ended up doing most of the work for the sake of completing the project. But at the same time, I couldn't put all the blame on the students that underperformed during the project. The main person to blame was myself. I failed as a leader because I didn't handle the different situations correctly, despite having struggles with social communication. In addition to group issues, we also had issues in getting the scope of our project approved. Our client for the Capstone project was the City of Sanford, Florida. This was historic because it was the first time that the City of Sanford was a participant in the Capstone program. They wanted us to come up with the proposal to help senior citizens use Uber as their method of transportation. The Uber Pilot Project allowed citizens in Sanford to use Uber for a discounted rate. We worked on the proposal of a brand ambassador program, which would consist of ambassadors helping senior citizens in terms of how to use Uber within the city limits. The challenge was to get the project done in only 3 weeks since the scope of the project was approved late by Uber and the City of Sanford. This caused a change in the roles each participant was going to work on, which brought more challenges for the entire group. Again, I ended up doing more than what was expected as the leader of the project. Despite this, again I cannot blame the others for the setbacks in the project. Regardless of my disability, this cannot be used as an excuse for failing as the group leader. Because of the failure to handle situations with the group participants, I was wondering how I could have a business if I couldn't even lead a college group effectively and efficiently. Despite these roadblocks, we eventually were able to complete the project on time. Our final Capstone presentation was one of the longest in the history of the degree program, but it was met with great reviews, especially from the City of Sanford. Because of this, we were invited to do a summarized presentation of the project in front of the City Commission of Sanford, Florida. The presentation was on December 12, 2016, two days before graduation. It was again met with excellent reviews. I don't know how we were able to successfully complete this project, despite all the setbacks and challenges. What is important is that it was done, and we got an excellent grade in Capstone! Overall, I was able to get A's for all the classes in my final college semester. It was done, it was finally done!

CHAPTER 30: THE TRIUMPH: GRADUATION!

Finally, the day that I have been waiting for has arrived! On Wednesday, December 14, 2016, I finally graduated with a bachelor's degree in Business and Information Management with a 3.7 GPA (Magna Cum Laude honors). After being told that I was not coming back to college, after all the struggles and everything that had happened in my life up to this point, all of it had led to this moment. This was not the ultimate life goal, but I was finally able to accomplish an important milestone. Not only had I graduated, but I was also recognized as a student graduating on the Autism spectrum. It was surreal to stand up in front of thousands and thousands of people at the University of Central Florida Arena. The president of the college mentioned my story, recognized me for my volunteer work, the Capstone project and graduating with the bachelor's degree from college. When they offered to do this recognition for me, I was not sure if I wanted to do it. The reason for it is that up to that point I didn't want to disclose my Asperger's and just wanted to keep it hidden. Reason for it was that I didn't want others to know about my disability for different reasons (employment, using Autism as an excuse, etc.). I was mostly concerned with being hirable in the marketplace because if I put on a job application that I had Autism, I would be rejected for a job. I didn't want to be in a situation of unemployment because of Autism. However, at the same time, my advocacy work for people on the spectrum continued to grow, and I began to feel that I had a responsibility of helping those that have challenges in the spectrum to achieve a greater life. I wanted to do something to help everyone in the spectrum around the world get the opportunities for them to live a much better life. That is why I accepted the proposal to be recognized. This recognition, in the end, was not for me. The recognition was for everyone that not only had Autism, but other disabilities in the world. It was to show to society that people with Autism and other disabilities are not a burden or a liability. It was a recognition that serves as proof that people with Autism are capable of living great lives and make the difference. The goal of the recognition was a call to take significant action towards creating key programs to help people with Autism to achieve a more independent and successful life. Also, Seminole State College did a news article about my recognition at the graduation, the Capstone project, and my work in the Autism community. Not to mention that the Orlando Sentinel also did an article about my accomplishments. The triumph was here, and I was able to demonstrate to people that had wished me the worst that I came here to make a significant difference in the world and that their wishes were not going to stop my mission. This showed me that I could accomplish much more in life. I don't know what was going to happen, but I knew that this was just the beginning. It was on me to achieve a greater life. My time is now.

WITH MOTHER AT BACHELOR'S DEGREE CEREMONY

WITH FATHER AT BACHELOR'S DEGREE CEREMONY

BEING RECOGNIZED AS A COLLEGE GRADUATE WITH AUTISM

THE ROAD AHEAD (2017-PRESENT)

AN AUTISM UNSCRIPTED LIFE

So 2016 ends with me getting my bachelor's degree from college. The one area, however, that I failed again was making new friends. In this college, I struggled with forming new friendships. Despite the ongoing challenges, Seminole State College of Florida was a great and rewarding experience. The degree was not set to truly help me completely with entrepreneurship, but at least it would help me at the end in accomplishing my ultimate purpose. Momentum was on my side after graduation. However, the year came with the same and new challenges. We start 2017 doing a job search and trying to become more independent in my life. I knew what my goals were, but I was struggling in getting there. I didn't have a clear mind in terms of business and what to do. In addition, I didn't have any experience in investing. And again, I didn't really have a strong network of contacts and friends that could truly help me. I wasted too much time applying for jobs that were not even going to help me in getting the skills necessary to start and run a business. While I was doing this, I was working on finding ways to create passive income from business, investments, and other streams of income outside of a job. It was frustrating to me that I was wasting time in a poor way and was struggling with my goals. I was confused as to the way towards accomplishing my goals.

This led me to find a temporary job that could help me with my finances until I got into the best situation to success. The first job I got was as a "Sales" Management Trainee with a loan company. But the position was misleading because it was a loan specialist and collector position. So I left after only one month. But looking back, this is a job I should have stayed more time after seeing what came next. Because of the struggles that I had in this job and because of bad advice, I decided to just pursue a customer service role instead of sales. The next two jobs I got were at call center positions. This was the first time I was working in a call center environment. It was different from the face to face environment that I was used to. I was focused on dealing with multitasking calls and dealing with angry customers on the phone. Not only was I struggling but I was not learning the skills necessary towards building a business. Not to mention that the pay was not enough to move out. That was the reason I left one call center position after being there for three months and went to the next position. But it paid slightly more, but I was spending more money on gas and car commute/wear. Again, I was facing the same issues at the job in the previous call center. I was also feeling that I was wasting time because by this time I had a more clear vision in terms of what business to work on or, so I thought.

While doing these jobs, I focused on working on my business on the side. In early 2017, I got connected with a business coach. He helped me in getting clear on business ideas, and I then proceeded to work on one of the ideas from the list. The strangest thing about this idea was that I thought about it back in 2010-2011. While I looked at my journals, I thought about building an organization that would help people with Autism. I don't know why I didn't act on it back then. However, since I have been with non-profit organizations since 2014, I now had a broad perspective about Autism based on personal and work experience. I wanted to do something to help adults on the Autism spectrum. The reason is that I saw that there was a lack of awareness and services for adults in the spectrum. I didn't know how exactly I was going to do it, but I knew that I had to find a way to do it. I tried to work on a business plan. However, I was struggling with the aspects of the business plan such as finances, organization, how to charge for the services, and what we were really going to focus on. I was able to do a market research survey to know the true needs of ASD Adults. I was doing all I could to get this project going. However, I was still behind. Then I thought that perhaps I need to take time off from working a job to fully focus on the business. Then, I left my third job in the year. After this, I was again struggling with the business plan. I didn't know what else to do, and I was getting into depression mode because I was trying and failing with my goals in life. I had thought that by getting back into personal development back in the summer of 2016 that finally I was going to go on accomplish my financial freedom and have a fulfilled life. However, in the area that I have struggled the most, I was failing over and over again. That area is making real-life connections with people. One of the goals that I set out to do in 2016 was to create a network of friends and connections from around the world. I used websites like meetup to go to different events and tried to meet up with people, and I had some success for a short time, but it still didn't work. I even tried to get into network marketing (which I thought about joining in 2010/2011) to meet like-minded people, but that still didn't work. No matter what, I was not making real friends.

Despite 2017 being a challenging year, I did some good and important things. First, I was able to go to Star Wars Celebration 2017 in Orlando, FL, the same place where Star Wars Celebration VI (2012) was held. I went all four days, and I had a lot of fun and a blast. I was able to see George Lucas in person again, and for the first time, I was able to see Harrison Ford in person!! This was during the 40th Anniversary Panel for Star Wars during the first day of the convention. Not to mention that after the panel, I witnessed a live Star Wars Concert with the one and only John Williams! It was surreal to be in the same room and at the same time with my idols, just like the experience from Anaheim in 2015. Even though the experience that I had wasn't as historical as Star Wars Celebration Anaheim, It was awesome to be there all four days in the Star Wars Universe and have a great time with fellow Star Wars fans. The only drawback, again, was a failure to build new friendships and connections. Also, during 2017, I started to volunteer with the ASD Adult Achievement Center (an organization that helps young adults with Autism) as one of their program assistants and fundraising coordinator.

AT THE NATIONAL MALL IN WASHINGTON, DC

Another important event during this year was that I was able to increase my presence on social media and internet. I created my own YouTube channel and brought in material, talking about Autism and helping other people achieve their purpose in life. Also, I created my website and starting to write blogs in 2017. In addition, I started making online sales on eBay. In early 2018, I was able to get full time employment in management.

My focus now is to work towards achieving time and financial freedom in my life. Also, I plan to travel the entire World in the coming years. Even though my life is not where I want to be at this time, I truly believe that I will achieve my ultimate purpose in the end.

FINAL WORD

So there you have it. This is my unscripted life with Autism. It has been a journey from the moment that I was born up to the present. I was non-verbal until age 4, and even after it, the struggles with verbal communication continued during elementary school. It did get better, but I still have my struggles from time to time up to this day. I have always believed since I was a child that there was something different about me, even though I didn't find out about Asperger's Syndrome until age 14. My greatest challenge has been and continues to be social communication and relationship building with people. No matter what; I had difficulty in relating to people, especially during my school years. I was dropped out of the special education program in the second grade because my verbal skills improved significantly and I was able to function "normally" with the regular kids. I was able to survive after being cut out of special education, but the challenges remained. I was bullied by others because of my way of being. Despite this, I was focused on not letting my problems control me and was able to complete my first key accomplishment, which was to graduate from high school. For the longest time, I blamed my condition for all the problems of my life and because I was struggling and wanted to be normal.

However in recent years, I began to accept my Autism, but at the same time not let Autism control and determine my life. Despite having Autism, I was able to work in jobs that required multitasking and required intense social communication, customer service, and sales. Despite social communication challenges due to Autism, I was able to go to networking events and go meet business people. Despite Autism, I was able to lead a team of 5 college students towards working and completing a project for an entire city and able to present it in front of the city commission. Despite Autism, I was able to come back to college and graduate with my bachelor's degree in 2016, being of the one of the few that have graduated from college on the Autism spectrum. Despite Autism, I have been able to help make a difference in the community from the very first volunteer job with the "Para La Naturaleza of Puerto Rico" to being a board member of an Autism organization.

AN AUTISM UNSCRIPTED LIFE

Today, instead of seeing Autism as a liability, I have learned to see Autism as the greatest asset of my life. Just because people say that I don't look like a person with Autism, doesn't mean that I no longer have it. I still deal with the challenges that come with it every day. It's just that I don't let it control and determine my life. Autism has given me a role of a life of service to others in society. In other words, it has helped me to fulfill a mission of helping others in the community. Even though progress has been made in terms of programs and services to help people with Autism in childhood, there is still a lack of awareness and services for adults with Autism. Society needs to know that Autism doesn't end when you turn 18, but it is a lifetime condition. Despite this, we don't have to allow Autism to determine our lives.

My focus is to continue to advocate on behalf of people with Autism, especially adults, for better programs and services that will help them achieve a more independent and greater life. Regardless of the function level, every person with Autism has an important role to play as the agents of change that the World truly needs. As you saw through my story, I went through a lot of challenges. You also saw the struggles that I went through in solving those problems. I may have been able to overcome some of those barriers, but today there are others that are in the spectrum that are going through these same struggles in their efforts to live a better life. Regardless of the function level, people with Autism need the opportunities to demonstrate to society that they too can achieve and do great things for the world.

In conclusion, we must continue to raise awareness, accept people with Autism as integral members of society, and take significant action towards helping those that are on the spectrum to have a much better life. I challenge everyone in the world to focus on Autism Purpose every day. Let's work together in creating a society in which people with Autism can make a positive and long-lasting difference in the world.

THANK YOU!

TONY HERNANDEZ PUMAREJO

ABOUT THE AUTHOR:

Tony is an advocate for people with Autism and other disabilities. He graduated with his bachelor's degree in Business and Information Management from Seminole State College of Florida in December 2016 with 3.7 GPA (Magna Cum Laude Honors). He was recognized by the president of Seminole State College of Florida, Dr. Ann McGee as an example of resilience through his work in the community and his educational and work accomplishments as a graduate on the Autism spectrum. In his final college semester, he served as the project leader for the capstone project, working with the City of Sanford, Florida, in regard to the Uber pilot project.

He served on the board of directors at the Autism Society of Greater Orlando from 2015 to 2017. He also volunteered with the ASD Achievement Center as one of its program assistants and fundraising coordinator.

Tony currently writes a blog at his website: https://www.tonyhpuma.com

CONTACT:

Let me know how I can help you!

If you have an inquiry or would like to submit a speaking request, feel free to contact me at: tonyhpuma@gmail.com

YOU CAN FOLLOW TONY AT:

Facebook: https://www.facebook.com/tonyhpuma

Twitter: @tonyhpuma

Made in the USA
Monee, IL
17 February 2020

21787813R00060